L-vis Lives!
Racemusic Poems

Kevin Coval

D0062009

Haymarket Books
Chicago, Illinois

Published in 2011 by Haymarket Books
PO Box 180165
Chicago, IL 60618
773-583-7884
info@haymarketbooks.org
www.haymarketbooks.org

Trade distribution:
In the US, Consortium Book Sales and Distribution, www.cbsd.com
In Canada, Publishers Group Canada, www.pgcbooks.ca
In the UK, Turnaround Publisher Services, www.turnaround-uk.com
In Australia, Palgrave Macmillan, www.palgravemacmillan.com.au
All other countries, Publishers Group Worldwide, www.pgw.com

ISBN: 978-1-60846-151-6

Cover design by Brett Neiman.

Published with the generous support of Lannan Foundation and the Wallace
Global Fund.

Printed in Canada by union labor.

Library of Congress Cataloging-in-Publication data is available.

10 9 8 7 6 5 4 3 2 1

Praise for Kevin Coval and *L-vis Lives!*

"Kevin Coval is a new, glowing voice in the world of literature. He writes—indeed, speaks, for it is his voice we hear singing. It is a bleak and dangerous time for all mankind. And yet we shall, despite horrendous evidence, prevail and survive— and hopefully grow as we glow on hearing his eloquent tribute to our species. In Kevin Coval's voice is our hope for a new world of peace, grace, and beauty."

—Studs Terkel

"This book is bold, brave, and morally messy—twelve rounds of knock-down, drag-out shadowboxing against a shapeshifter. The dark humor, intellectual fervor, and emotional rigor Coval brings to bear animate these pieces, turn caricatures to characters, implicate us all. It's about time."

—Adam Mansbach, author, *Go the F**k to Sleep*

"Coval's greatest strength is his rhythmic, beautiful prose . . . he's relatable and likeable for his remarkable honesty and boyish romanticism, his studied understanding of race and class, his unflinching faith in hip-hop culture and his willingness to speak truth to power, no matter what the personal cost."

—*URB Magazine*

"At turns lyrical and fierce." —*The Onion*

"A prophet . . . a tour-de-force . . . he can soothe and scathe, hurt and heal, in the course of a single poem." —*Providence Journal*

"The figure of the whiteboy at the center of *L-vis Lives!* is a beast of line-beat-breaks, an ambitious and naive thief, equally loved and dissed in his unattainable odyssey for Black cultural props. Kevin Coval rips the Black skin off hip whiteness. Part Norman Mailer's *White Negro* ("urban adventurers who drifted out at night looking for action with a black man's code to fit their facts") and part social aesthetic-activist (but branded a terrorist) determined to continue the *Unfinished, Collected Works of John Brown* . . . Kevin Coval may not have wanted to but he has proved, at a time when many poets use metaphor and restraint to tiptoe around the tough issues of identity and borrowed race, that most L-vises (especially the ones falsely hardened by their own often rejected love of hip-hop) have Soul."

—Thomas Sayers Ellis, author, *Skin, Inc.: Identity Repair Poems*

"Kevin Coval's poetic novella teaches us the traps of life, allowing us to love our reflections, filling us with the joy to live, to struggle for life. The world is ours."

—Vijay Prishad, author, *The Darker Nations*

"Tough and smart, real and surreal, aching and funny, in-the-tradition and startlingly original, the trials of L-vis show us the challenges of giving up on whiteness—a process at once monumentally hard, too easy, and absolutely necessary."
—David Roediger, author, *How Race Survived U.S. History*

"Coval echoes Ginsberg in his spiritual revolt and longing for multicultural transcendence. Funny and empathic . . . his well-stocked poems contain earth and spirit, body and soul." —*Booklist*

"Kevin Coval's *L-vis Lives!* is an unstinting excavation of race and culture, art and ownership. It offers poetic affirmation of Ralph Ellison's signal insight, stated forty years ago, that 'whatever else the true American is, he is also somehow black.' Though some, out of either optimism or ignorance, have dubbed our nation 'postracial,' Coval reminds us that America is a country in which race is always receding from but ever returning to the center of our consciousness. With poignancy, humor, raw insight, and no small amount of soul, Coval has fashioned a poetry for the present. His voice demands our attention."
—Adam Bradley, coeditor, *The Anthology of Rap*

"This book reminds me the if anyone can save this world it will be the artists and poets. It is through their efforts that we really understand things, much more than just by knowing the facts. Through art and poetry we can understand other realities and experience them through all our senses. This book explores the complex meanings and motivations of cultural appropriation of Black culture by white youth in America. Like many whiteboys who have felt the aesthetic power of Black culture, hip-hop being the most recent form, Kevin Coval has followed his desire and admiration to emulate the creators of the genre without losing himself. By loving and honoring his idols, and studying hip-hop culture and the context from which it emerged, he can imagine himself walking in another's shoes. And by acutely observing himself and his own responses, and those of other artists who have crossed over, he has been able to analyze the American racial dilemma more deeply than most and to see what a country in denial refuses to see, that white supremacy is alive and well in America . . . Perhaps only through writing as honest and lucid as this, through art as perceptive, can we ever come to terms with our history."
—Henry Chalfant, producer, *Style Wars*, and photographer

"Kevin Coval, Chicago bard, inspired teacher, and Pied Piper of poetry to a generation of hip-hop urban guerrillas, does with *L-vis Lives!* what good art demands: I was in orbit." —Bill Ayers, author, *Fugitive Days*

Contents

death side

broke/////////beat/////////intermezzo

whiteboy i could've been:
a suite for John Walker Lindh

for Lisa Arrastia, Shradha Patel, & Idris Goodwin
for always keeping it real
for always keeping it real / with me
for always keeping me / real
for all these years / for real.

Mediocre artists borrow, great artists steal.
—Pablo Picasso

Once they hear you it won't matter what color you are.
—Mekhi Phifer's character, Future, in *8 Mile*

*The price the white American paid for his ticket was to become white
. . . This incredibly limited not to say dimwitted ambition has choked many a
human to death here: and this, I contend, is because the white American
had never accepted the real reasons for his journey.*
—James Baldwin, *The Price of the Ticket*

*I got to thinking how many records you could sell if you could find
white performers who could Chapter play and sing in this
same exciting, alive way.*
—Sam Phillips in *Rock and Roll Is Here to Stay*

*Elvis was a hero to most but he never meant shit to me
you see straight up racist the sucker was simple and plain*
—Chuck D, "Fight the Power," on *Fear of a Black Planet*

Hearing him for the first time was like busting out of jail.
—Bob Dylan

Acknowledgments

big ups and immeasurable thank yous to the readers of the manuscript at its various stages, for all y'alls' suggestions and tough cuts and real talk, you are the home team, quite a crew: Roger Bonair-Agard, Idris Goodwin, Adam Mansbach, Lisa Lee.

shout outs to Parneisha Jones, Adam Bradley, Patricia Smith, Thomas Sayers Ellis, Bill Ayers for the love, the words & the belief in this project.

the idea first came to me after a long-ass conversation with Billy Upski in like '99 though he don't know it.

good lookin out: to journals and anthologies that have published various versions of these poems before.

wanna say what up to my little brother Eric, a whiteboy who's been there for all the rising and falling—who always has my back.

Haymarket Books: what can i say—Anthony, Julie, Sarah Mac, Jon, Rachel, Ruth, Bill, the whole team. it's a humbling thing to have others risk and believe on your behalf. to put it on the line for the lines you craft, the line you walk.

and for s.dot—i wrote a lot of these poems next to you, or with you in the next room. you believe more than anyone. all your work shows me that. i see you. i thank you. i love you.

and for you, reader, it is quite an odd privilege to share this with you. i really do thank you. each word. each line. i am grateful you have found it. i hope it finds you / well.

Preface

this is an old story, depending on who you ask. here is Elvis Presley, Vanilla Ice, Eminem, me, the Beastie Boys, and other whiteboys who consider themselves down, mashed into one character: a contemporary L-vis, a whiteboy who uses and misuses Black cultural production, who is at times appropriate and who appropriates, who blurs the line and crosses it carelessly.

this story starts at a mistake, of sorts, an american anomaly that has become cliché: the whiteboy drawn into and reared by Black music, who then turns practitioner (to whatever degree that is possible—a whiteboy practicing Black art). L-vis rises to stardom, struggles, succeeds, falls, offends, takes, steals, invents, gets props, is dissed by white people for being drawn to something other than white, something other than phil collins /grateful dead/country music, gets dissed by Black audiences, gets (too much, many would argue) love from both.

L-vis is a sincere artist and a thief. L-vis is naive and poor. L-vis loves the music and covets the cool. L-vis holds the spectrum of hero/anti-hero and human complexity. you may root for L-vis and be antagonized by him. he may be like you or your son or friend or that white kid who tries to flee the community of his birth. he is, at times, something like a genius, an idiot, a false idol. Elvis Presley, Vanilla Ice, and Eminem rose in a Black musical form and brought that form to a larger white audience. all three, reportedly, tried to kill themselves.

this is an american story, epitomized in the life of John Walker Lindh, the so-called american taliban. a kind of L-vis, a whiteboy with a story like mine, who listened to and was politicized by hip-hop music in the 80s and 90s and knew much of what america stood for and proclaimed, much of what our parents and teachers and politicians said was doublespeak and deadly. communityless because of the lack of authentic discourse on race in america, Lindh, like many of these whiteboys, like many who fit into an L-vis archetype in american culture, became obsessive and skewed, but dead on that something about this country, its history and continued maintenance of systemic racialized preference and superiority, is unconscionable and worth fighting to change.

this book hopes to broaden the conversation, to raise questions and not have all the answers. there is something about this whiteboy, this L-vis character who *knows something is terribly wrong*, who knows america has a racial complex and intimates consciously, subconsciously, at times courageously and often incorrectly, that a way forward into greater under-standing is in visiting and hanging and learning and participating in the public cultural space of the other.

of course, with some of these L-vises, their participation leads to a bastardization or muzakified version of the original—and for some, a financial reward much greater than the rewards received by the inventors and teachers of the style. and this too is the american story, a grotesque history of capitalism's exploitation of Black cultural production.

L-vis draws a lot of attention, deserved or not. in the same mo-ments he delights and troubles our imaginations. he is what is possible and what is problematic. he is very much alive in our history and cultural imag-inings. he is not at a campground in wyoming or at burger king bathroom in the wisconsin dells. L-vis Lives! at the center of the american experiment. this is his story.

Introduction
by Patricia Smith

Out loud I'll say it: I grew up on the west side of Chicago. Yeah, that's the part of town everyone tells you to stay away from—during the Great Migration of Blacks from the South to the dream-burdened deceptions of the North, the West Side did a passable imitation of the Promised Land. Black folks were steered directly from the Delta into its rumbling factories and boxy tenements. They were crammed in until a sprawling slum was assured, until breath became an impossible. (Now, as if the community's delicious proximity to downtown were a newly discovered secret, lofts and ludicrous rents are slicing their way westward. That is, however, another story.)

Growing up in the Chi, I lived in a courtyard brick-upon-brick apartment building on the corner of Washington and Homan. The building had an overhang jutting from its southern side, a concrete outcrop that served no discernible purpose—except that it gave us a cool, dusty place to play when Chicago's summers grew insane, with temperatures hurtling into east hell. We crouched in the shade, tossed jacks and jumped doubledutch, making up mildly pornographic quatrains while stomping rhythms into the dirt.

Lawndale, our little slice of the West Side, was, by design, almost 100 percent Negro. I say "almost" because I remember one white family, withdrawn and tentative, but there—holdovers or pioneers, I was never sure. I never saw the adults, although my mother had. But I did see the son, whose name escapes me if indeed I ever knew it. He was "that whiteboy," skulking at the edges of Garfield Park, defiantly riding his bike down the center of the boulevard, casually introducing us to his penis.

Indeed, that was that whiteboy's schtick, the thing he was known for to keep from being known for simply being white. He'd set up shop under the overhang, rooting himself in the most shadowed corner, then he'd tug down his Wranglers to reveal the smudged and pink curling/uncurling thing. And his price was reasonable—he charged a mere dime to look, a quarter to touch. For many of us, it was our first introduction to the penis, which we had not yet connected to any activity of a carnal nature. It was just weird. As I said in a recent poem dedicated to this long-ago slum entrepreneur: "and if not for his / clipped command, *next. next.* we would / not even notice him attached to the thing."

Imagine the long, snaking line of giggling colored children, quarters in their fists. And that whiteboy, making a niche for himself, knowing instinctively that the key to acceptance was to peel himself raw and display the ultimate vulnerability. It never occurred to any of us—even the tough boys who were making their mark on West Side streets—to pummel him for his difference, because he brought us a particular magic. Beneath that overhang on Washington Boulevard, he presented his qualifications, and we folded him into the music of our days.

I hadn't thought of that whiteboy (damn, if only I could remember his name) for years, but, unbeckoned, he peeked at me from the last page of Kev Coval's *L-vis Lives!* a brutal and biting glimpse of how culture carves and reshapes us. I'll admit that whiteboys who so slickly appropriate, who find a Negro niche and cram their whole selves into it, who masterfully mimic the hip dip and the swerve, who shame me with their unerring knowledge of dark language, who spin and spit and bust lyrics wide open—I'll admit that I'm mesmerized by their naked need to inhabit the other, to throw aside pomp and privilege and wallow gleefully in the gutbucket, to wear labels like "wigger" with a skewed sort of pride. I know that that long-ago entrepreneur who flashed his roscoe for cash money had worked long and hard (neither of which he was) to flip the American dream and marvel at its underbelly. He was going to be one of us even if it meant showing how he was most unlike us. He played the card he had, and the game was acceptance.

I bet I'm not the only person who thought Kevin Coval was Black. Hell, he's so chilly and unflappable I don't even look hard. He argues loud with Black folks about Black stuff, and sometimes he wins. He strides past in his vests and hats and cigarette slims, and I see the sisters giving him the appraising side-eye. He is an undisputed master of the lyric drop, a hip-hop historian, and every word he speaks has the brand of languid street drip that can only be earned by beatdown or blood. When I heard, I think through a poem of his, that he is Jewish, I instantly conjured some unimaginable hybrid, dashikis and yarmulkes swirling in some rainbowed nether-region, and the harsh reality rendered him no less Black.

They are curiosities to be ridiculed or embraced, but no one really talks about them, these white men of color. No one considers their origins or the source of their craving. They pretend race means nothing when it is merely everything. They risk alienating the culture they are shunning and the one they seek to adopt. The one damnable thing they can't change is their skin, which glows like a pesky beacon no matter how soulfully they speak or spit. No one has bothered to label this pursuit of Blackness a meaningful tribute or a persistent dysfunction. Beyond their novelty, the we they do so well, no one really knows these whiteboys. There's a reason I don't know the name of the charmer who pocketed so many of my quarters.

This is a relentless book, brave and uncomfortable, an unflinching introduction to the wavering mindset of that "brutha" we pointed out and danced with, the one who taught us how we were supposed to walk, the one we stared at, eyes wide and mouth hanging open, as he swallowed stories we thought we owned and spewed them back as rhyme. In this book, we hear him speak, sometimes halting and unsure, sometimes haughty and entitled. We step every wicked step with him as he examines who and why he is.

Nothing like this has ever been written. *L-vis Lives!* is a cultural touchstone, a book that will easily move into a space that's been waiting for much too long. Time for scholars to clear their throats. Time for the poets in the bars, waiting for their moment on the mic, to argue feverishly over their tumblers of tequila. Time for Kevin Coval to face the madness, to realize the funky bag of snakes he's unleashed, to find root once and for all for that odd boy out in the club, the one who sweats silver while his hair refuses to nap. Now I'll know why he aches for the soul of the other. Why the soul he was born with just isn't enough.

life side

L-vis is a baby in the wilderness
after Frida Kahlo's Girl with Death Mask

i was born a skeleton taught to wear the wolf mask.
i stand on the prairie and retreat into the mountains.
i am a baby bearing flowers. i wear a pink dress but
i am a skeleton taught to wear the wolf mask.

ten fingers, ten toes, two arms bearing gifts, history
behind me, in the mountains. i am on the prairie, a baby.
i bear flowers in a pink dress and bone bonnet, my head
fit for the wolf mask, but the flower i brought is yellow.

we can tear its petals together on the prairie. it is my prayer
this will carry me till i learn to sway right beneath the drunk
moon. for now i am the sun, set to rise in Blackness, till i can
wear the wolf mask and roam the plain(s) assuming all is mine.

the crossover

it was the end of disco. all the jobs were moving or changing or drying up in the city like the river after a summer of no rain. the parents moved farther from the city or themselves or their families for those jobs. hours in commute. we received a key to let ourselves in after school. they would not be home till late. sometimes they would not be home at all. sometimes the commute was too much. the parents too far gone to see each other. busy running around. sometimes running around with other parents. sometimes running around doing things parents shouldn't do.

there were plenty of tvs and radios. there were older siblings. city/suburban sleepover camps. there was a black friend. a new york cousin. a late night pbs airing of henry chalfant's documentary. there was a leak. it was run dmc. it was newcleus's *jam on it.*

the house was quiet. peanut butter spread on crackers. sandwiched potato chips. there was bruce lee, saturday afternoon shoguns. kamala the ugandan giant. nothing was explained. no one home to contextualize. everything was mixed up. ninjas wore black like ice cube. burn hollywood. the sleeper hold. the college radio political talk show said south africa.

there was apartheid at the schools. apartheid in the lessons we sat thru. nelson mandela was in america. his name was chuck d. his name was krs-one. what is a Black Panther? there is apartheid on the bus home. there is apartheid in the lunchroom. the sides of the city we don't visit. were told not to. there is apartheid on the television. bill cosby aside.

there was a tape deck. a walkman. there was no apartheid in the music. no separation in the library. books endlessly check-out-able. there was holden. the hero Huey P. the wandering protagonist in the midst of all that quiet. the new music to soundtrack the walk to school. the music truthed. the music was middle finger fuck you. fuck you actor reagan who sent uncle dave crazy back into the streets. fuck you actor reagan who warred on the drugs my mom did. what you know about three jobs and two kids and running from land-lords. the music was solace and ammunition. alone and one in the chamber.

i listened to every word. memorized all the words. recited the words into a notebook. there was not a viaduct in the music. there was not a neighbor-hood to avoid. there was not a gunnery filled with columbus broken prom-ises. there was not a cold war of white flight and divorced unions. there was a hero. for the people. all of the people.

i wanted to be a hero.

Posing

in a full length mirror
on the sliding closet door
of the bedroom i share
with my brother, in the town-
home my mother rents in the suburbs

an X-cap tilts / over my shaved head
like an unplayable pinball machine.

nose still too big
for my face. chin hairs
i'd call a go-tee
struggle for articulation.

i look hard

i am shirtless
in a Raiders Starter™ jacket,
belt strung thru loops of 38/34 jeans
pools of denim wade
at my tim-less ankles.

every muscle in my body
wishes it were Bigger.

Jealous of the Black Boys
a love song

they always looked polished.
high tight bald fades, creased
pants cuz they mama made em
iron early before school.

always fresh dipped.
not cluttered floor
crumpled jean, three day
dog smell and dirty.

they smelled like rain
ıı rubbing alcohol.

royal blue Chuck Taylor
fat-lace spaghetti heaven.

they talked slick, quick or slow
always cool, like they inherited
their daddy's invention.

call and (tepid) response

in my mother's kitchen over a bowl of frosted flakes
it clicked. something i'd been contemplating for weeks.
i called Marc Cohen immediately and told him
he should run for class president and i would be his campaign manager
and introduce him to the eighth-grade student body
by kicking a rhyme.

it was 1988, rap had yet to hit the shopping mall.
Marc was a bit skeptical, but every night of the campaign week
i worked on writing and more important how my mouth looked
in the mirror when words came out.

by thursday night i was a minute fifteen seconds
of mostly Grandmaster Melle Mel mimic at the end
of *Beat Street*, his eponymous elegy for Ramon (rough!)

but in the early hours of that friday morning
when birds kicked a symphony in the trees
near my window in the subdivision of pheasant creek
i thought the end needed something more, something
to move the crowd of thirteen- and fourteen-year-old
north shore, majority jewish assimilated, upper-income kids
who liked wham! and def leppard. i dug into my growing crates
of memorized bits and *ah-ha*-ed when the b-side of The Fresh Prince
and DJ Jazzy Jeff's *He's the DJ, I'm the Rapper* tape popped
into my head like a toaster pastry.

the morning was pre-AIDS Magic
showtime in the all-purpose room
a cafeteria with a stage, hundreds
of chairs facing the podium. giggles
and whispers whipped the air like crickets
until Mr. Feely, the industrial arts teacher
and 8th grade class advisor, unfortunately
named considering the rumors about his wood
shop after school, introduced the candidates.

Marc was in the middle, like Monie Love
but before he took the mic, i entered stage left
commanded the crowd clap their hands to a beat
which didn't exist, but all the emcees started that way
and it's true, white people are like a bootleg rolex
we can't keep time. but i rode the jagged rhythm
four-fifthed my way thru the written verse, monosyllabic
heroic couplets regaling the virtues of Marc Cohen: *the funny
kid i've know since grade three / we wrestled at my house
he rolled in my dog's pee / but we got older / got tough, got bolder /
got to be Jr. High residents / make some noise for your next class president*

admittedly the crowd kept quiet.

but you don't stop the body rock
and i didn't have enough good sense
to exit, i wanted to make Wood Oaks Jr. High
bounce to this, take all our mid-puberty
bon jovi loving energy and make the roof fire
at least spark a bit, a modest bbq wd've been nice.

i wanted the cafeteria turned into church
at least what i thought church might feel like
a church in wheaton maybe, but still not bad
for a room full of jews.

undeterred i went into my appropriated call
and response: *ladies, all the ladies, all the ladies
in the house say Marc . . . say Marc . . . homeboys
make some noise let me hear you say Cohen . . .
say Marc Cohen . . . say Marc Cohen rocks
the spot, everybody . . . Marc Cohen rocks
the spot, a little louder . . . one more time . . .*

and in reality a few friends perhaps
raised their voice above whisper, but
in my head i was baptized, a head
ready and able to move the crowd.

Faded

the stylist at Michael Anthony Salon
has got no idea what a fresh cut is.

a step, a bowl, a bald wall
straight-lined over the ears
like my head wuz a topographically diverse region n shit.

for prom i wanted to get a peace sign shaved in the back.
i went to Quick Cuts™ in the strip mall on dundee rd.
the barber was frail n divorced, dirty blond
thirty somethin, her fingers smelled
like Kools. she just put a restraining order
on her second husband. said she'd give it a try.

> when i got home
> n looked in the mirror

> pac man.

> a mercedes
> hood ornament.

> no fuckin
> > peace.

the white train

L-vis (in)fantasizes after watching *Style Wars* for the 26th time

parades boroughs like royalty
rumbles pristine over boulevards.
in guarded railyards sleeps
razor wire german shepherds, watchmen
defend lay-ups, flashlights
all night eye the virgin
yet to be sprayed colored mist
yet to be defiled by hands wild
with style.

under steel thrones, they gather
gaping chaste snakes teasing in
and out of the neighborhood.

they dream of bombing
benign skin, writing funky
fresh names the length of its body

destroying all lines
defaming for fame

the herd of unheard
catching wreck.

L-vis (dis)covers the blues

one night, after dinner fight
grades down like his attitude
L-vis huffed out the bungalow
like an asthmatic, tears and snot
a sweet and sour dessert in his mouth.

hopped the bus he was warned against
the one that crossed the side of the city
Javaughn, Durrel and most of the guys
on the team lived. he'd never been invited.

last stop; a street he'd never seen,
a strip of currency exchanges, hair
salons, storefront churches, corner
store conversations like foreign
languages, mothers' stern voices
corralling children home. metal carts
carrying groceries, laundry, or scraps
of construction, depending
on who was pushing.

he gazed down side streets
filled with men in front of tools and cars and coolers
music twisting out factory issued stereos like yarn
caught in the trees and pigtails of little girls riding
pink-streamered bicycles on the sidewalk
white tires rolling over chalk rainbows.

and then he saw:
fenced-in black
top, hands beat bricks
to a beat. headz bent
& nodding. talk fast
body part base
line, stories over boom
bap. words picked
up like passes. ran with
however long
one's breath
will carry them

black studies

cuz willie perdomo

black is the color of my true love's hair
black is the color of all i care, black records
black stax, black bodies stacked, shack(il)led
by o'neil english. speak back, black backs
lashed raised scars, africa attack, black oil
black guns in the hands of blue, black foils.
blues black serum, black sermons, black sirs
ma'ams, black surgeons, eugenics ebonics
black persons, black-eyed susan, black gruesome
most fear when black fester, black grew sons
spores, black moors, black muslim round black
ka'bah tours, what black for? black spades
dig black earth, black words i learned

to speak
first

solo tip

at night
i mimic
the art
of the illest.
i am sick
with it.
the dis-
ease of word
nimble.
an adroit
i flex.
a writer
-in-apprentice
to the Masters
of Ceremony
who séance
my histories
in rap syllable.

L-vis trip/tics thru american history class
after pat rosal

I.

g-d must be an english teacher who likes irony
and master tongues. a creator of slipcovers, i guess
create is a strong word, perhaps supplant is sufficient
like the new testament and what not. all of this built
on atlantis and choctaw. g-d must like clouds a lot
considering he is said to bat cave there, a resort
among the light and billowy. clouds remind me
of rabbits. rabbits scare easy and burrow into holes
and scamper all over the forest and fuck a lot.
g-d must like to fuck a lot so america made tuskegee
and immune deficiency. barbie the apple headed
wishboned from walt disney. adam smith quarters
the garden into enclaves, robert moses parts the bronx.
america must think it was typecast in g-d's biography
on network tv, a big budget and eminent domain.

2.

emmitt smith ran for 18,355 yards
the most in nfl history / he ran
most on sundays / g-d's day /grid
iron / metal / rust / industry built
war /mongered / mongrel sounds
walter mondale / half majestic derek
jeter / jesters / dick gregory / albert king
rodney / jesse owens on a sparrow branch

rickey henderson / stolen base / swollen
face / emmett till could not run fast enough
at 14 / july 4 / the candles are roman / pies
black / buried / snow / cones and levities
re /mastered / on a white / label

3.
letter to al jolson
i will place you in a wooden box
near the mirror i change in front of.
you crooned in burnt cork, i will not
have to. you one knee whistled mammy
i will sorry mama thug a tale so churned
it will sing sweet butter in my mouth.
you wore the mask so i may rock the fitted.
you movied with aunt jemima, i will don
the do-rag. i get faded but black hung
in your pores. its ashes float in the blood
river. i honor your death pyre in memphis.
i upstreamed the mississippi like salmon.
crossed the atlantic in black vinyl to cess
pool in the short lives of beatles and stones.
your legacy: monster pack rats, we carry
crates of alan lomax ethnography. we dig
you like sick(le)/cells we can't jail. break.

L-vis imagines if Tupac had read Etheridge Knight's *for black poets who think of suicide*

he woulda crossed the Brooklyn
bridge, grabbed B.I.G. and squashed
beef with the Hebrew Israelites
over BBQ tofu and corn bread.

he woulda lived.

he woulda sought a sit down
with Cornel West and Sonia Sanchez
had the Hughes brothers stand up
from their beatdown and shoot
the movie version of Robin Kelley's
Freedom Dreams.

he woulda just married Jada.

he woulda excised that Bishop
in him, and become a trumpet
for Black warriors not a commercial
death row sentence for young, Black
and ghetto, a video game cartoon
where the wildest exit quickest.

he woulda been poet laureate of Oakland
and got around and around to more schools

where fifth graders recite his words like Langston
and fifteen-year-old girls recite his words
like church, keepin they head up in front
of a mirror that refuse to see them.

he woulda pulled suge knight's card
said no more work selling Black death
no more work with fbi, cia, no judas
no brutus, no leviathan.

he woulda lived
a trumpet raw horn
ghost screaming
from the grave
of lost records.

cracking the code

the kkk has got three-piece suits
Ice Cube

shvartza was easy.
my grandfather yelling sundays
at the football field cuz men were
end-zone dancing and making millions
to get their heads bashed in. he was
bruised by a similar work force, but died
in debt with no dance at the end
of his run.

downtown meant dangerous if you lived in the suburbs.
then suburban kids moved to the city their parents left
and the city became *the north side*. the south side a forest
we were never to enter. *public schools* were no door bathroom
gang fight graffiti crack dens. *welfare*: Black babymachines
with headscarves and packs of kools, no jobs or fathers in sight.
Section 8 housing: Cabrini Green candyman, food stamps and ebonics.

the code grew subtle.
east pilsen is safe and artsy. *west bucktown,* an emerging neighborhood
erasing Humboldt Park. anything raw, unexplored, unpolished, unrefined
desolate, dark. you may find riches if you are there early, if it is the next
hot thing, if you are willing to pioneer.
avoid anything *public*: housing, education, transit
avoid anything *immigrant*, migrant, anything with labor.

the code becomes gesture:
knowing looks, slight nods, a clubhouse
whisper, wondering if they will pull their pants up
by the bootstraps, everyone else did
what is wrong with *them*. all this in the meeting of eyes
following the mention of Allen Iverson
a rapper, someone young and rich and Black.

the code is coded in its decoding.
i have Black friends, am liberal, marched with King, voted Obama
guilty OJ, Barry Bonds, an asterisk. a kind of nostalgia, a return
to innocence, before tongues were bit. when words freely flung. guns
and no taxes, rage simmering became relaxed laughter, a joke
about the ghetto, it being torn down, the lie of *mixed income*
when only condos will rent and townhomes will sell, all this
an evolution of language, a slang of separation. they do oral art
physical primitive, ancestral, folk, urban, multicultural, diverse.
all veneer and drywall to maintain the pristine of white.

rep.resent: L-vis tells a white lie

I

where *you* from is the first question.
the foundational opening and aesthetic salutation
in a cipher, a club, basement, gymnasium
bootleg your-guy-works-at-kinko's-and-makes-free-flyers-type-parties.
the answer more than an impressionistic determinate, you might know
their cousin or went to high school with the DJ, you could tell
how they would rhyme, what graf artists they saw, what mix tapes
or college radio shows they listened to. on the south side
JP Chill on WHPK, on the north side WLUW's Hip-Hop Project
all low-watt end-the-of-dial 80s fm frequencies.

but no one came from where i was from.
three kids in my high school liked hip-hop:
me, my brother, a seven-foot, hundred twenty five pound kid named Jamar
who transferred from a private school in the city cuz his parents
wanted him to play basketball but he wanted to play cello and had a crazy
early curfew. so i'd roll solo and when asked   i'd mumble . . .

2

look. money magazine named my suburb
america's best place to live.

my mumble turned
into a different city, an alternative state
an unauthorized autobiography. i never lived
near Black folks. the closest thing to a gang

22

was my little league team. but Miami seemed
dangerous compared to the cul-de-sac.
the mumble turned into a myth and i belonged
and mumbled so much i believed
and wore that shit like a shield
made of melting plastic.

it wasn't cool, Ice
i kept saying to myself
knowing i'd get burned.

fresher than them

He seemed very lonely and had no real friends.
He just didn't seem to be able to fit in.
Red West, All-Memphis Football Player, Elvis's lifelong friend

what the fuck i wanna be white for?
you're white Jay, and you're corny as fuck.
Danny Hoch as Flip Dog, the Montana Gangsta Blood Thug

work boots & dungarees
polo shirts & sweaters
khakis & blue blazers
they're squares.

i had a black & pink drape
coat, white loafers & black
shirts with houndstooth pants
they'd call me squirrel

or freak
or wannabe
i was
none of these.

i was fresh
voice, a new
style, singer
wantin to song.

L-vis explains the white do-rag

after Cornelius Eady and Greg Tate

an appendix. wisdom
teeth. naughty by nature's
vinroc. what purpose
do i serve?
                    wave cap
for a placid ocean. a nap
in a haystack. an afro pick
for ricky schroder. the rodney
king tape. what use am i?

                    yarmulke
for a traife g-d. dunce cap
cool. lunch counter soda
jerk segregationist. pointless
beanie of a klansman. a 99¢
style rocker. a crown of burden
i can always leave behind.

snaps!
L-vis learns to play the dozens

your mama's so white she powders her nose w/ cocaine
gets free stuff at the grocery / dainty crackers n goat cheese
so white she got a supermarket in every subdivision she owns

your mama's so white she got seven dwarfs cleanin her castle
mirror yes men on the wall tellin her she the fairest / so white
princes wage war over her glances / troops murder in her name
n men get hung / jus by whistlin in her direction

your mama's so white she disappears in a bowl of sugar
beneath sheets / she's casper / klan maiden / so white
bread named after her / milk pasteurized complexion / so white
she married all the presidents / g-d make christmas
snow fall light like her blanket of skin

your mama's so white she hates her black mammy
denies her ethnic roots / bleaches hair eyebrows
pussy / so white she paint her picket fences bone
she live on cloud nine / so white her kids movin
back to condos on clouds six seven n eight

your mama's teeth so white they look like the supreme court
clarence tom jus the gap in the middle / so white your mama
think food stamps the latest black cartoon at the post office
think government cheese a head start program

your mama's so white she gotta magic marker a tampon to know
what to pull out / stands on crystal staircase ceilings lettin domestics
clean her diaphragm / so white / she a ballerina twisting
in a music box / you can't tell when she's smiling

your mama's so white her tears are diamond / blood ever clear
carbon monoxide breath / your mama so white she kills herself slowly
like dickinson plath woolf chopin characters rotting in secret
rooms / eating fenfen bonbon soap operatic anorexia / so white

                her insides stank
                her face is plastic
                and can't crack
                behind all that shit
                she's holed up
                inside

The Humes High School Band
Presents Its Annual Minstrel Show

it was amazing how popular i became after that.
elvis presley

it was a thursday night.
much of the school turned
out to see dancers, twirlers, a xylophone
trio, barbershop quartets and comedians.

the air starting to sweat
this april in memphis.

he borrowed Buzzy's red flannel shirt.
buttoned it up all the way to the top.

he never played before an audience.
just some ballads for girls he strummed
beneath an oak tree, sitting on a park bench.

his brow hot from the flannel, all that make up
caked on in the parking lot.

he was not nervous.

backstage
an assistant to the director said good luck.

he said thank you ma'am
but what i do don't need luck.
the globes of her eyes fluttered

he walked on stage
whispered his Black-
faced voice into a silver
microphone. all the white
girls sighed and screamed
and knew their fathers
might not be okay calling
this white Black boy
dreamy,
calling him
king.

quarters in the
    don't play arcade

Joe Strummer points to the Future

the fans in Philly were unruly. rude
boys in leather imitating british blokes
imitating disenfranchised Jamaican toasters
who wanted recordings of nothing but Motown.

these punks pierced in shredded denim
wouldn't listen to Cowboy, Kid Creole
even Melle Mel had trouble moving this
crowd, now throwing bottles and slurs.

Grandmaster Flash, a child of the West
Indies, stayed cueing records in his head   phones.

        the kind of kid to play
        with his food. pidgin
        peas on his mother's table
        always found their way into
        the rice, over bacalao, though
        he remained skinny he loved
        the kitchen. brought turntables
        there to mash vinyl, whisk beats
        in the two bowls of his eardrums
        until the blend was so perfect
        origin undetectable.
                he always thought the sound
        systems of King Tubby and U-Roy
        an unfulfilled universe of circuitry, a simple

switch, he learned to mix at St. Catherine's
Vocational HS on 168th St., a set of skills
obsolete in a deindustrialized Bronx
in the dawn of computers. Flash cut
wire, fused cords of base amps, found
a light switch could make records talk
to each other in tongues and polyrhythm.

Joe Strummer was pissed.

a child of Turkey, thief of Dub
punk's Woody Guthrie, lead
singer of a British band who debuted
on America's bicentennial.

he grabbed his beer once he heard
the riot emerging from backstage. asked
Scorpio for the microphone. the band
of second-wave skins listened to Strummer
a g-d in a cult of anarchists.
he spoke to them of Flash, the wheels of steel
industry grinding to a halt, *this is the sound
of the world changing*, he said. *shut up the fuck up*

and listen

I am Mr. Freeze!

he could go in any Black or Puerto Rican neighborhood
and walk through and say I am Mr. Freeze
Ran Dee, *Boogie Down B-Boy*

the first & only
whiteboy w/juice.

a postindustrial accident
when he fell into the rock

steady mix. mad inventor
of electric boogie. in the lab

eating, drinking, thinking:
b-boy. running against the wind

umbrella in hand like workers
riding bombed trains when it rains

hands in white gloves
like Marcel Marceau

he taught the moon
walk to Michael Jackson

kept the real physics for himself
pausing inertia mid twist

frame captured, contorted
suspended gymnastic

the body a bridge
from Queens to the Bronx.

the old pantomime elevated
in the streets on cardboard

or concrete or green top, hand
ball courts in the park. public

mimic of the new war
on drugs and the poor.

translator of egrets floating
around Lincoln Center.

Solid Gold, Flash Dance
fire starter. part responsible

for popping up a million
will be b-boys & b-girls

w/ the body possible.
physical limits knocked

down like dominos
the world   over.

Bill Ayers in the Kitchen

undoubtedly there are greens
on the stove. greek olives, hummus
rich, white cheese on the table, a fine salad
with red and yellow tomatoes.
a pasta maybe with pesto
two bowls: one with chicken
one for vegans.

people will pour in all night.
Studs Terkel read *Working* on the back porch.
Edward Said sipped tea in the living room.
bread has been broken, made and thrown
by the smart and courageous and unknown
organizers and politicos, poets and other
dancers, educators by the class load
most student groups south of Madison
have their start around this giant
wooden table.

Bernardine may be speaking
in another country or at the office
late surrounded by legal pads
and legal documents trying to forge her way out
and a way out for others

                       while a terrorist is in the kitchen
engaged in five conversations
with the earnestness of a schoolboy.

a trained Chicago improviser
who says *yes and*
and moves the conversation
to a future place where learning occurs.

this is the secret recipe:
the humility to learn anything
from anyone in the kitchen;
how to glaze salmon with pineapple chutney
or build a preschool or bomb, but learning
mostly how to talk at the level of human.

consider the inherited ingredients:
the seat of aristocracy, the private schooling
the boardrooms and bedroom suburb.

the wild and awake leave, Siddharthas of the 60s
with molotov bravado, a teacher first
holding a flower to america's temple
a flower that is a mirror, a giant metaphor
without casualty. a boom in the pentagon
a goon with big glasses, a peabody for pundits
and politicians on the television

but in the kitchen, considered
and contemplative, an open house
a guide and guru, a cheerleader for the left
and left out and lost, a chef for bandits
with band-aids and fresh berries. a man

who cooks to feed, sure, but more
to gather and galvanize, congeal
a movement some would say he is
partially responsible for
fracturing.
                    yes sir!

there will be cooking this time around
and stories and spices and mixing
elements and people and giant cakes
pasta salads, yes and
sometimes the flavors
come together brilliantly

this stew is homemade.
the cook is making
the party explode.

Rick Rubin's (Black) Magic Act

his mom would take him from Lido Beach, Long Island
into Manhattan to hang out in magic shops with old men
and learn the ropes, the patter, the shtick to say during bits.
they'd tell to him to practice in front of a mirror, if you can
borrow something from the audience: keys, a coin, a handkerchief.

in high school, the same trip. his moms in a Cadillac waiting
outside CBGBs on her only son, inside, digging the Ramones.
each tuesday at Negril's hip-hop night. the east village exploding
with future sound, Black in origin. the whiteboy, the jew listened
intently, a college student used to picking up from the masters.

his nyu dorm room became a laboratory. desks pushed together
to hold turntables, attempting to mash scenes thru the speakers.
the desire to connect the city, Uptown and Downtown (Ayin & Malkut)
a party he threw with the Treacherous Three and Heart Attack. the need
for a community to validate all this freshness. that old longing

for dropping it on the one/ness. the trick of borrowing something
from the audience and incorporating it into your patter/n, now
everyone hears something recognizable and something foreign
and what kind of magic is that, to reposition, to collage, to make
new and nostalgic. a ton of black vinyl lifted and recompositioned
something borrowed for T LA Rock's It's Yours, the world is / one
giant LES of sound. up rock and down beat in the same dance
floor. NY / the center / the world / a Danceteria / a club for swindlers
pill poppers and lockers, Blondie and Fab 5 Freddy, a polyglot rock on
a punks' come up, a magician in front of mirrors freaking this trick just right

death side

L-vis is discovered

@ the museum of contemporary art.
the big show/casing hip-hop acts
from all over the city. venues like this
never put on local talent but tonight
doors at 7, show at 8. by 6:30
300 people standin outside.

everyone n they cousin came
w/ demos. ladies went shopping
on Madison for outfits. girls w/ hair
like ropes n roots got they nails did.
so many tims on the corner cd've been
a boot camp click reunion. dreds n white girls
reeked of musk and music seeped out
the museum's closed doors like dank
spreading till everyone got whiff
and the sidewalk became soul train.

a night like this seems like a movie
everything worked: folks flirtin, jokes
fit into conversation like new socks
glide into all-white kicks. history
will be written tonight. air
so clear—it's camera ready.

nerve

He never seems sure of the proper accent to adopt
AllMusic Guide's review of Vanilla Ice's *To the Extreme*

knees knocked so loud the first row thought a clave
was added to the band. sweat drips thick like old honey.
dry heaves side stage near the curtain, a couple of hawks
into the tin before my name announced. it sounds foreign
at this point, something distant. then a rush under lights
a gallery of unknown faces glare, they have paid to be here.
they have decided on this night to be nowhere else
but in front of me . . .   listen (please):
i will sing my songs.
i am doing what i love.
it is not my own invention
perhaps it will be
at the Grand Ole Opry
but i really want Black
audiences to feel me
cuz i am making Black
art, and am not. i am
something new and am not.
i am authentic and not.
all this every time i gyrate
in front of metal and electric
carries my voice thru the air
like murmur or murder.

this is my real voice and not.
i am fresh and tired and many
may never know the difference.
i think this is what i really
sound like, alone, the voice
that emerges in the solace
of pen. i write these songs
then stand here swaying,
my real/borrowed voice
singing.   i think

the cash register in Dr. Dre's head
goes bling

> *I thought he would be able to get away*
> *with saying a lot more than I would . . .*
> Dr. Dre

jimmy iovine pressed play in his beverly hills garage

                    and the tornado sirens moaned
in the trees, lightbulbs exploded into handclap casio synths
fuck you pay me mantras, twisting knobs in front of the soundboard.

Dre flew the kid on the tape from Detroit to LA two days later.

this is the fox of history smiling in the chicken coup
the Nile rushing north, cows butchering the butcher
wade in the water on *YO! mtv raps,* opposite day, the faint
hum of reparations massaged out worn hands in the field. it struck
him clear as lightning. he is no ben franklin, but this is just
what the doctor ordered.

robert van winkle has some tough decisions to make

there were two deals on the table.

Chuck D wanted to sign him[1]
have the Bombsquad work
production. if there was gonna be
a rap L-vis, he'd like to get paid
have a hand in the molding
this time.

and there was capitol records
and their million dollar signing bonus.
and Robert's foreign two-seat junker
at the mechanic. he'd never seen
that much negative space before
in the bellies of all those zeros

the mouths of six ghosts
macaulay culkin, frozen, alone.

[1] (i know, i couldn't believe that shit either)

the beastie boys cast a video
for paul's boutique

cabernet bottles, ounces of herb, mounds of cash
line the conference table, three upper east side boys

wear afro-wigs, inebriated grins. a fledging punk
band turned hip-hop by the downtown eighties and Fab 5 Freddy.

signed to capitol records, grown men, money to burn, casting
the *hey ladies* video at a los angeles hotel. coddled by television

they loved Rudy Ray Moore's bug eyes, watermelon, chicken bones
mercedes hood ornaments above their crib. silver blunts in their mouths.

near the Pacific today, a line of bikinis around a door, down the hall, flesh
paraded at auction for the boys who are beastly. for the boys behind

a conference table in afro-wigs. whiteboys in afros' wigs. they are not Black.
the joke is they are not Black.

L-vis is dating Jezebel

a dancer at his video shoot
brought her to his trailer
where a guitar lay
                Miz Jaquanda
he called her
strumming roots
music, even sang Negro
                spirituals.

he'll take her
to the *good* restaurant
in the hood.

he'll explore Black
sound, deep reverb
in those hips she swings.

he'll swipe her smile.
she'll braid his hair.

he'll speak of her potential.
she'll tell him he's stupid
                dope.

he'll bastard her patois
n ease through doorways.
he'll ask her on tour, to award shows.

she'll dress in designer lingerie, tabloids
taboo, matching tattoos, an opening
to escape the prison of *Jet Magazine*

Matando Güeros
L-vis visits the classroom

is Bitron's favorite death / metal group / he is a hulk
of a kid / chipped black fingernails / orange streaks in brown hair hang
at his waist a metal spiked dog collar / circles his neck / but sweet
his voice stuttering to find words

he's presenting what he's been thinking about / his family / the closed
factory / his dad worked in / his moms a schoolteacher in Mexico / cleans
homes / here / they grew up rancheros / had little money / less problems

he wants to move back / away from gangs and drugs / live on a farm
raise chickens / from the back of the room Daniel / head full of cornrows
says in all seriousness / *take me with you*

Bitron shares singsongs from his journal littered with skateboard stickers
shows books he's reading about socialism / Carlos Cumpián poems / Victor
Hernández Cruz / it's a good presentation but i tell him to write more about
his parents / Mexico why he's socialist not communist / less Dr. Seuss
more Bitron / i ask / what *matando güeros* means / nervous the other
Mexican kids smile / *kill the white people* / Mari interjects

silence stares around the classroom / like it's waiting for the answer
        Bitron asks
doesn't everyone feel like that

                sometimes

Vanilla Ice on the *Arsenio Hall Show*

vanilla ice: um i'm vanilla ice i'm not no elvis presley

arsenio hall: ahuh-ahuh . . . i know a lot of Black rappers are probably
angry because (turns to audience) some of the white people
screaming didn't buy rap until you did it, until they saw a
vanilla face on the cover of an album that probably makes
them angry because

vi: if it makes them angry, it's not my fault (high pitched)

ah: mmm-hmm

vi: did i have anything to do with that . . . ?

ah:

vi: no

ah: so they should dog the people, uh . . . he-haha

vi: no what they're daw . . . what they're sayin is they are showing their
own jealousy, man that's all it is. you saw flavor flav, you
know me and hims, . . . we're homies

ah: is that why you brought him out to show you have a black supporter?
and . . .

(crowd boos)

vi: no i brought him out cuz he's a friend of mine

(vi hears the boos, begins to smile and head nods approvingly)

they don't like that man, heh . . . (all smiles)

ah: that don't bother me, i'm not liked by a lot of people, a lot of times . . .

vi: . . . all right . . . me too . . .

ah: i say what i want to say . . .

vi: . . . so do i . . .

ah: because i'm an american and i have that right . . .

vi: word . . . me too.

(the crowd erupts in screams)

ah: you think that's gonna bother me?

vi: you think that's gonna bother me?

ah: no, don't phase me . . .

(screams dissipate)

ah: i ask the question i ask, i didn't see a purpose, it seemed unmotivated
. . . i wonder why you did it?

vi: i did to show that he's my homeboy, and he's in town and i'm kickin it
with him, and if, you know i'ma help him out like he helps
me out. knowwhati'msayin?

ah: i want to bring him out, but i want to bring him out when he's a guest, i
didn't know exactly why you did it though . . .

vi: surprise . . .

ah: i was ah . . . going to see . . . if you had an answer for me . . .

the critic truths: a found haiku

at the photo shoot
the makeup artist spreads base
on his foundation

L-vis wonders about the burn at his back
[in the voice of Neil Armstrong]

> *What's Duke Ellington without that swing?*
> Q-Tip

how cold is ice if it is destined to melt?
how hard is cubic zirconium on a wrestling belt?

i am leroy jetson
in a sliver spacesuit.
i moussed my hair
myself and don't want it
tussled. i am ghost
ridden. one small step
penned by four men
in an agent's office

what is chess without the checkmate?

what street cred do i deposit
if said street is lined in shrubs,
adorned with autumnal names?

is it a leap
to bedeck my body
in african medallions
if i retain the rights
to be the man?

if truth is fluid
i might not be
as cool as i think.
i can see my dracula
in the mirror. shadow
puppets in pluto's cave.

what color is my face when the base is all black?
what color is the sky, the night is all black?

what is the rep without the mutation?
what is the rent check on my occupation?

how can i be the first
man on the moon
in a zoot suit bought in Harlem
when i have always traveled uptown
to see the stars / burn?

dissatisfied with his costume,
L-vis invokes Nat Turner on Hollow-wean
A Battle Rhyme

i'm casper the friendly ghost
white rapper with offensive boasts

dub step snow dred lock rasta hoax
colonial selector affirm wonder bread toast.

yes, yes, i burn original most
blues source, Black host, scary to most

i am the greatest of all time
LL's a lip licking lame joke.

i am the real gangsta rapper
Ice Cube's the scapegoat.

after rappin run for office in order to take oaths
melt bootleg dukke chains to bathe in fake gold.

it's like i built a kingdom on yeast
the way my cake grows.

all style innovations, i track those
like bloodhounds chasin Harriet
in the underground of trapped souls.

macks official, Don Juan Bishop
pinky ring slam green Cadillac doors.
hands gleam in daylight, foot on the latch of trapdoors.

christ on a chariot the way fans follow my rap tour.
spit fire burn em all in the rapture

even though when i started rhyming i didn't rap sure
didn't want to say any bad Black words

but i spit up the culture i consume so all i say is Black words
Jesse James of slang the way that i jack verbs.

casper's ghost not friendly cuz casper's a cracker
risen like smoke on the lawn where the cross in the patch burned

ghosts have returned, i am hoping the mic
in my hand will kill em / while i'm waiting on Nat's turn . . .

letter to white backpackers
and battlerappers

there was a time when this was not ours.
before whiteboys told off-color offbeat
punch lines on the mic and called it rap.
a time before Atmosphere sold out
the Metro and every suburban kid
disobeyed their parents who like
their parents forbade rock & roll.

this is so much like rock & roll.

this has little to do with Em
and his record-sale misogyny
and more to do with Dr. Dre
and his relationship to Interscope.
more to do with Rupert Murdoch
and his son buying Rawkus.

there was a time before hip-hop
got named, when no whites wanted to visit
the cities they abandoned (unless they got left
there for being poor, too).

there was a time when there were no whites
in hip-hop. when it was Black and Brown
park jam freedom centers, collaged funk

sneaker jumpsuit, gazelle glasses and gang wars.
there was a time white kids were scared
and out of place, unsure if we'd get beat
in a basement of busted speakers

there was a time when you had to take two trains and a bus
even to buy a tape that didn't have phil collins bon jovi
run dmc bootlegs on Maxwell St., before
bubblegum counterculture indie-underground downloads.

it wasn't safe to be white in hip-hop
at least we imagined, cuz clearly it wasn't ours
and maybe people thought we were Black, but no one
ever said anything about us being there.

the only white dude on stage was the sound guy
and he looked like the iron maiden night school mechanics
who called you wigger and did kick your ass behind White Hen
with steel (not shell) toes cuz too much bass bumped out your walkman.

there was a time when you had to be asked to a party
otherwise you wouldn't have known it existed, a secret
world you were let in on, cuz someone handed you a flyer
or told you what time to knock on their cousin's back door.

there was a time when there were no whites
in hip-hop but when they came, they came like Warhol
Malcolm McLaren, Tommy Mottola, Cecil Rhodes
ready to oversee, define and bottle all that noise.

there was a time before hip-hop
got named, when white folks hung Black people
for speaking and dancing and drumming like this and this
is the denotation our skin shines, brightly when we enter

a culture that is not our own. a culture that is a celebration
of life we disturb and deaden and shackle and legislate
against its existence. our whole lives, predicated on controlling
life that morphs and hides and tricks(ters) us into thinking
it's just music.

photo collage / jump cut-ups: white mobs in 1956

there is no vacuum, though we'd love to sell one.

while teeny boppers poodle skirt, shimmy and pat
boone their way through watered-down versions of the twist

their parents saturday in straw hats near a cornfield, the edge of swamp
khakied and short-sleeved button-downs. the wives dress for tea.
eyes scatter, unfocused as if the branches were bare.
there are hankerchiefs sometimes unfolded from a back pocket
not for tears but crumbs. there is food here. picnics is the term
eni-meanie-minee-mo-catch-a-tiger-by-his-toe-if-he-hollers . . .
there is slow here. a-nothing-is-wrong-and-retribution-impossible-
kind of gait.

the streets and valleys beneath hotel windows.
the gorgeous pits of rows before the stage filled
with shrieking girls dressed for the last day of their virginity
glossy photos and permanent ink pens, hands pleading
for air, faces frozen in craze, mouths wide enough to swallow
anything. there is excitment, panic, flight or fight, a condition
of confinement . . .

the parents gather at the feet of Black boys turned effigy
ugly beyond their own parents' recognition   *smile*
skinned and strung, just some regular young boys

or older men, or perfectly perfect and ordinary
but always Black. their whole lives wronged
by white people whose children gather
in front of a whiteboy turned Black
totem. they are screaming and crying
at the feet of this white
boy, they wash
in tears.

can we believe this is their cosmic lament
the inverse mourning of Black bodies swinging
in front of their parents, as this whiteboy's hips swung
wet into eyes of white girls

are they weeping
for gnarled hands and charred flesh and sliced genitals
stuffed like apples into the mouths of princes, for this king
of rock and roll, of public sex, of jump

does the wind down the road blow stench into their throats

are they hysterical for the history we inherit
and perpetuate and live in

are they pushing on police barricades to practice
for the coming revolt

holla for Troy Davis
after L-vis reads the 3rd section of "Howl"

i'm with you in county

        where your mug shot is a clown mask

        and there is a circus of villains selling

        cotton/crack to the front row seats

        of your sentencing

i'm with you in county

        where boys are incarcerated as men

        in this new jacked up city of kickback thieves.

i'm with you in county

        where many have been coerced into confession

        chicago knows burge and long nights of blue torture.

        we know folks get knocked for holding steel

        and the steel mills that used to hold gary

        no longer health care.

i'm with you in county

        where Nate is

        standing in front of ten boys

        he shares a floor with. D cell, it's called.

        he is trying to read a poem about his brother

        shot and killed four months ago. his brother

        who will never come back. the whole room; the ten

        boys, some parents, teachers, even the guards

        for a minute of their lives, everyone holding

        Nate, who is weeping like a mikva bath / holy

        water for a minute and a half, he brings the mic

        to his mouth but his arm is an avalanche, but

the words we needed rose like dust but didn't
bring Nate's brother back or Nate home.
we're waiting for so many to return
millions now in the US
the largest prison system in the land of free
we're waiting on you Rooster
caged bird with majestic feathers
your sister stays singing the sunrise
since you left and the block holds you
and remembers
and forgets
we're waiting on so many
so many who will not come home
so we're with you in county
where you are
in isolation twenty-three hours a day
holding a vigil and garage sale for justice
we're with you in county
waiting for you to come home
at the lake with a full plate of bbq
and peas and rice and a razor blade
in the morning croissant of the DA
arsenic in the starbucks of the judge
or at least dramamine or blood
or a least a jury of peers, rights
written by slave owners upheld
for once, for someone
not eligible for white.
we're waiting for you

to come home and kick it and teach it

and be about it, cuz we are trying to

be about it and we rally around you

as symbol, but you are person and flesh

and locked twenty-three hours a day in isolation

and we are here via train or car and some rode a bicycle

and what kind of leisure does that sound like

from the inside

but we're with you in county

despite the distance and hours of sunlight

we're with you in county

desperate for hope and progress

your case so clear cut, all the eyes

have recanted your name and the real gunmen

walk factory floors of berretta and congress

we're with you in county

where your words bend rivers

where you live on the inside

shining, despite all that darkness

and opaque bullet proof plastic, you

too supernova, too galactic / historic

to not reach us, your bottles we collect

in the living room of the future world

we're with you in county

where there are thousands like you

who need someone to be with them

we're with you in county

where the air is laden with death

but you rock a fitted halo titled with bravado

like what now blues, what now history
and its shackles, what now executioners
we're with you in county
where you're already free
of this country, this body
we're with you in county
and want to be
free   like you
want to be home
and we want you
and want the world to want you
like we want you

free.

white art

after Amiri Baraka

poems about birchwood are bullshit
unless forests of mercantilists burn
tied to tree trunks, skin smoldering
trail of dental records, inheritance
in flames   motherfuckers
kicked in the nuts postulating posturing
tweed tenure track post-poetry impostors.
we want poems that dance around the ear
machete and tech 9 pressed against the temple
poems that will kill someone / tonight: demigods
false idols, crack donald's hall of mirrors
no horses head genocide   just assholes
squeezing gates of definition tighter. they
never get fucked. they only give department head:)

we want poems that tie billy collins to a chair
and beat him. we'll see how pretty, witty and meaningless
it all is: a million stanza march ready to flood his organs
alternate multi-cult cannons shoved in his paternalism
backfire prosody until his blank eyes black

we want poems to stop lying
in showers of middle-age heartbreak &
cancer. fucking grad students ain't noble.
poems that grab *new yorker* subscribers
by their neckties, hang them in Morning-

side Heights, Harlem, West Wicker Park
River North, University Village like piñatas
summertime shooting galleries, gentrified
chickenshit wax-that-ass museum displays
of quaint colonialists discovering a cafe.

white poems about whiteness devils & white
powder medicine men. poems that stole everything
we own & won't surrender. 40-line reparation pathologies
to jazz-writers who beat-bopped a century of plagiarism
who beat-box between line breaks, who cop language
break /ups and think they in   OH!   /vading

white poems / little dick slavery poems
blueprints rolled on the table in daylight
poems that cut school funds / a(f)firm
white woman ass/imilationists, dic-
tion bigots, cracker gun barrels, white poems
w/ mathematic inconsistencies, voter fraud
interest-rate hikes, redlines & red stamped
bank loans. poems that smother children
in knock-off handbags & nike shoes
poems starved for attention. a white poem
that destroys a white world that eats itself
rather than consume the Other   finally
a poem that will grab the king's keys & stab
fair maidens and game wardens repeatedly
the royal court bloody, shocked & clawed.

hero to most

i am a hero
to most. the great hope
of something other.
a complex back-story.
something other than
the business of my father.
bland's antonym.
jim crow's black sheep.
the forgotten son
left to rise in the darkness
among the dis
carded in the wild
of working class, single
mother hoods. a hero
who transcends
who translates the dis
satisfactions of the plains:
kids of kurt cobain
method man amphetamine
the odd Iowan who digs dirt
and lights beyond the pig yard
spits nebraskan argot.
hero to the heart
land, middle brow(n) america.
relics of metal
and rust, punks
in the five and dime

who sag their pants, mouths
filled with burnt jargon
heads wrapped in polyglot:
somewhere other
someone else, i am
a hero to most
who hope there is
something more

L-vis sittin on some New Magellans

i remember this one show in Oslo
where the crowd went nuts and i felt
like my life was a dream
Eminem

i put more english in the mouths
of nonspeakers than a british general.
seventy thousand fill stadiums and know
the words to every song even if they don't.
the government should pay me.
i bring midwest Black vernacular
like beads and animal skin. trade
tokens in the language of marketplace. dialect
glass encased. studyable. i am
a linguist presenting my findings in the field
of Black labor. alan lomax anthropologist
liberal apologist. the logic of Blackface.
europe gets me cuz they rumbled thru Africa

too.

Indonesian kids dig me like coke.
this is what neo means. i'm a bazaar
of wares, knickknacks decontextualized.
i could hawk wood sculptures from Senegal
even if they were manufactured in maquiladoras.

i am perceived as authentic cuz my bio reads
poor. this is the language of the dissed
and dispossessed: vowels drop like school budgets
consonants contract like fine print. i study books
like an accountant.

i'm clownin

the reason i bleached my hair platinum
was to match the other metals i alchemized.
i was just fuckin around on e pills but Dre
said i was baby face fresh and Africa
would recognize. i am the american
child freewheeling in the culture
candy store. see me
the life i've (re)created
into a dream. merrily
merrily

ode to painkillers

when the head aches too bad.
sleep is like some rumor of sleep.
shows. shows. when the wake must go on.
how else do i climb down this mountain
hop out the train of these tiny bottles.
i've become accustomed to picking cotton.

the first sip of bourbon is enough
to know i will cram a week into last call.
i will not go home. i will not go home
alone. at all. i will be chauffeured to friends'
homes who house glass tables filled with candy.

i have a sweet tooth and bed of novocain.
i have a chemist's heart and license to practice
medication. i am sick and too tired to tire.

i am clark kent
refusing to change
out his superman.

national anthem

i have been so many versions of the minstrel.

my law suit is at the cleaners.

the sample i've been sued for
birthed death
row, i am gangster
incarnate, responsible for murder
many times over.

it is 1994.
this seems right.

two years from now
Pac will be killed.
hip-hop will be
hard and unhappy
after me. serious
business. i made
serious money
for serious corporations

there is nothing more
gangster than taking
over culture you don't
have the language for.

millions make for isolation
fans or dollars.

i am sitting in the bathroom.
the door is closed. i am alone.
i cannot page anyone.
those who would know
how i feel
are gone.

i came back rasta and knotty
nobody wanted me.
i returned fat and sequenced
the big ass of every joke.
i am sitcom in syndication
the archetype of a whiteboy
in a black mask.

40 oz.
of vodka. hands full of white
pills

i am after the cold
war. the bomb was never
dropped. i am a glasnost
baby. Nas is right
the world is mine.
there is no one
to fear but my own

reflection
in the crowd
at my shows
a mosh pit
of farm hands
pulling phantom
triggers of rented uzis.
they listen to me and NWA.
they will become prison guards.
they will never be what they want to be.
they will never be all they can, b

this is the real
national anthem.
the song of everything
stolen, everything
confused and borrowed
mixed and the myth
of the pure, rotten. original
is doublespeak, is Orwell
is the hands behind my back
signing contracts. the masses
of stacked records, stacked bodies
unpaid Stax samples, stacks of books
i jacked from the Schomburg
get returned to the library of congress.
the Black frat anthem i snatched
now the sizzle of national airwaves.

i am saying
this is the truth
the real national anthem
the song of everything stolen
i am saying
there is something terrible/ly wrong here.

i was in a spacesuit rocketing to the moon
a minute ago. last week i woke stomach pumped.
i am drowning in a pillowcase of blunt wrappers
the truth
is i love this music
my best friend is Black
and gone
i am alone and all that
behind this bathroom door
there are millions on the other side
fans, dollars and otherwise.
i am saluting the flag
like it's August of 77.
i am on a solo tour
with a bottle in hand
behind this bathroom door
i am cold

as ice.

returning to Memphis

you can't forget the sweat of a southern bathroom
deep canyons of wet where huge roaches live or

the sweet funk of burnt bar-b-que wafting
from roadside shacks like recently bloomed iris

this is a tale of two cities.

upon returning they tell me
not to go to the southside.

they tell me this in every city i enter.
at least not at night, not too far south

not past the Arcade, a greasy institution
with runny grits and sweet potato pancakes.

the bus boy is from the southside
he sits at the counter. he doesn't clear tables
just refreshes water and turns his mouth
to the sun till his silver grill discoballs.

murder capital is a dubious badge.
it keeps shifting between here
and Chicago, though northsiders
have no reason to believe this is true.

beale st. is a drunken disney world.
bachelor party puke and $10 parking.

memphis is trying to breathe
life downtown: condos, lofts, boutiques

it is a ghostly walk alone
beside these rigged cafés.

driving old memphis and midtown
who would want to leave the mansions
and strip mall pole dancing classes house-
wives shake their moneymakers in dreaming
of elsewhere and loved by someone other

i sang songs for them from beneath my birth name.
singers today adorn themselves with this alienation.

T-Pain; T for terrible or troubled or tolerable. Akon
a con.
this city
the same since i left it.
the same since i sang in it last.

i'll say this:
the hipsters at sun studios give a good tour.
the girl with blonde curls wore cowboy boots
had a historian's certainty and kind southern twang
Jerry Lee Lewis would find majestic.

what i'm trying to say is Kings die here.

The Lorraine Hotel
is still intact. it was not burned.
a woman in the parking lot
is asking for change. she is
not visiting the civil rights museum
today. she has come for change.
memory does not buy white
bread or sheets or rock or the moon.

the balcony looks like Jesse is still
there pointing at ghosts. where
a thirty-nine-year-old King fell, white
towel over his super-novaed face, there is
a wreath that looks like the wheel of a ship.

an advertisement in the early fifties
in a Black newspaper read: *vacation
and recreation without humiliation.*

but in truth the Lorraine is more motel.
pull in, pull up southside open-air balcony
no air conditioning, southern spring heat.
front office with soda machine. not a room
at the Madison or Peabody palace downtown.
i never offered the guesthouse at Graceland.
but a small twin bed, vanilla curtained room
at 406 Mulberry, where once word got out

it shot around the filling stations where all
the Cleaver boys and three named, simple
syllable fellas came hunting with guns.

the south has always had a thing for burnt flesh.

dry rub houses and homemade hot sauces
an experimental type of funk.

Isaac Hayes recorded *Black Moses* on Stax
down the road, south of here.

i changed my middle name to how Aaron is spelled
in the bible cuz i wanted to speak clearly.

Moses stood on a mountaintop and saw the promised land here.
he might've been forty or four hundred years away

it's hard to tell
how far we've come

but i mean this
Kings are killed in Memphis
city of burnt flesh and charred meat
stench that lingers like bullet holes

the history is so funky
we think it's sweet

try to memorize and museum it.
call little rock newlyweds and texas
nurse conventions here, chevrolets
stuffed with midwesterner camcorders

the history is so funky
folks lured by its sweet
but it's just flesh
memorialized, smoked, rubbed
burnt stench floating down
the Mississippi.

broke/////////beat////
/////intermezzo

what the whiteboy wants

the whiteboy wants
to be liked
wants not to be
thought of
as weird.
the whiteboy wants
to be dug, felt, thought of
as fresh.
the whiteboy wants
his name
synonymous
with dope.

//////

the whiteboy wants
critics
not to underestimate
his name each time
it appears on a bill.

//////

the whiteboy wants
you to scream
if you are with him
wave your hands

wants girls
to cry and their fathers
to worry. the whiteboy
wants to be consumed
on the charts
in the streets
in your heart-
throb

/////////////

the whiteboy wants
the ladies, all the ladies
and a woman to understand
him in the morning

/////////////

the whiteboy wants
day to pass
in a white cloud
of percocet and xanax.
the day to disappear
and sleep before sunset
the whiteboy wants
night to be all black
sky and glitter
stars and sequins

////////////

the whiteboy wants
a company, a crew
to accompany, a band
a brand. the whiteboy
wants his brand/name
uttered in tears
and ciphers

////////////

the whiteboy wants
to be wanted
on the radio
in Nashville
Ed Sullivan's Show
Steve Allen
the Knitting Factory
Fat Beats

////////////

the whiteboy wants
to be the only one

////////////

the whiteboy wants
the cool and hip

of a leadoff hitter
in the Negro League
quick & slick
with the steal

//////////////

the whiteboy wants
a room full of people
to want and know him
wants a room full of people
whether it be Madison Square
a Vegas stage or the Hawaiian
comeback concert broadcast
on NBC, the whiteboy wants this
room to be everywhere he goes
all of the time.

the whiteboy doesn't know
this to be impossible.

//////////

the whiteboy knows
something is wrong
thinks answers might hide
in the darkness
cuz the light lies
like a motherfucker

////////////////

the whiteboy knows
his father lies. learns words
too early like affair and colony

////////////////

the whiteboy knows
knows the bookshelves
are crumbling beneath the weight
of whitemen's lies

////////////////

the whiteboy knows
Black jokes. he tells Black jokes
to the one Black boy he meets
at summer camp. the Black boy
makes the whiteboy's nose red

////////////////

the whiteboy knows
there is something wrong
with all he has heard

////////////////

the whiteboy knows
all he knows he wants
to unknow

//////////////

the whiteboy knows
he would never move
his body if not for basketball
b-boy up-rock

//////////////

the whiteboy knows
he would've never left
the house and went to
the library unless Chuck D
used big words n dropped
Bobby Seale out his mouth

the whiteboy knows
he would've never left
the house if not for the open
mic all-city cross town hall
mecca

the whiteboy knows
he woulda stayed right where he was
if not for Black college radio djs

and Steniski playin all that
miscegenated mash-up

the whiteboy wants
to be special, to transcend
his race, the white-
boy wants to be John Brown
cuz that is the only whiteboy
in history worth being

the whiteboy wants
the next Jacob Lawrence
to paint him in a series
of lithographs

the whiteboy wants
to be brer rabbit & fuck
with whitefolks
or at least
the whiteboy
wants to be the whiteboy
other whiteboys fill
in the blank with
when thinking about
whiteboys
they want to be

///////////

the whiteboy knows
his existence is a goof
a synapse in the millions
of borders it takes to hold us
back. so the whiteboy feels
like an outlaw, a public enemy
too

whiteboy i could've been
a suite for John Walker Lindh

desire for the cipher

marin county
california
suburbs, usa

parents break up
white liberals lie
fairy tale lives
border patrol
fictions of the
Other.

here i am
isolated. i dream
a space, to be
where Others
see hypocrisy
and i can be
who i be

5%

hip-hop is a million doors
white kids might walk through
an invitation to slash ricky schroder
nancy reagan negations and hear
news exports from the brutalized, body
criminalized, masters
of ceremony—

some of us listen
in headphones, study
behind closed door
bedrooms, we share
with the silence
stalking our homes
like boogie men do
our parents' nightmares
afraid we'll let them
in.

posing

our blackness should not make white people hate us
John wrote in a chat room under the pseudonym *doo-doo*

at fourteen

every time

his computer

slept he stood

to see his reflection

glaring in the full

length closet mirror

behind his desk. he knew

he was not Black

but desired as we all

dream we are, something

                        Other

than white

picket fences

i have never seen happiness
JWL

parents flirt & fuck
vows of fidelity
& everyone
is in therapy
& yoga
& eats sprouts
& zoloft
& runs mountains
& companies.

hot tub dinner silence
can you pass the vodka?
        all the women
in my family are functional
alcoholics. the men great
teachers of deceit and desecration.

what does the whiteboy do
when he realizes everything
around him is a lie?

Suleiman al-Faris

i will shed this skin.
it is dirty. bland. you
can see blood whirl
through like a gutted
computer. a ghost
my skin, my name
the government
knows me
by.

i will become knight
of Solomon, reborn
re-visioned, my name
a shroud, re-alized like
Lord Jamar, KRS-One
Wise Intelligent, El Hajj-
Malik El-Shabazz

The Autobiography of Malcolm X

how many of us

             prisoners of privilege

             praying to betray our inheritance

has Malcolm saved?

not once, but twice, named.

prison to Nation to Mecca

servant of fire—

how many whiteboys

did he unknowingly (unwillingly)

light the rail to race/traiting?

self-sacrifice

all i have
is my body.

i will grow
my beard.

let hair mat
beneath skull

cap. all white
flowing suits.

i will walk
in the middle

of streets, reciting
Koran, arms out

as if on the cross
balancing my steps

between here
and there.

last letter home

i am going. you must have known this day would come. how could you
think it wouldn't? did you think we would stay lampooned in cul-de-sacs
forever? i have ridden my dirt bike to the other side of the forest preserve
and discovered John Brown and Haymarket and Weathermen and
Upski—texts you meticulously cover. the circles around your pixilated eyes
are ashy motes that will fire again. i am hip to your double speak. i have
been lied to. i am aware of this now. i am well / red in Marx. i have allied
myself with the proletariat who drive your cabs, press your clothes, slice
your kebabs, who silence beneath the weight missiles close on their
throats. there are many like me. i am leaving *with the intention of fighting
against terrorism and oppression, not to support it.* i have sewn your name
in my inner lip so you will hear the words of Allah fall from my tongue
like ripened fruit. i am leaving you. i am a patriot / act. gone. mad.

whiteboy still

why didn't you kill me!
MC Serch at the end of *Bamboozled*

more than anything else
this betrays me. i will not
be interned at Gitmo.

Yasser has no layer
i have a team. i will be tried
by peers. they look like me
at least. i am not guilty
though i ran with guns
against you. i am still
the whiteboy, my treason
unimaginable. america
will never consider
who would betray
all this

       skin?

Notes

"fresher than them" quotes from Peter Guralnick's *Last Train to Memphis: The Rise of Elvis Presley.*

"The Humes High School Band Presents Its Annual Minstrel Show": April 9, 1953, Elvis Presley performed at the Humes High School Minstrel Show.

"rep.resent: L-vis tells a white lie": After the success and criticism of *To the Extreme*, Vanilla Ice lied about his place of origin, a suburb of Dallas crowned by *Money* magazine as "America's best place to live."

"L-vis wonders if Tupac had read Etheridge Knight's *for black poets who think of suicide*" contains quotations from Etheridge Knight's "For Black Poets Who Think of Suicide."

"Vanilla Ice on the *Arsenio Hall Show*" is a transcription from a youtube clip of the *Arsenio Hall Show* originally broadcast on Fox in 1991.

"5%" refers to the branch of Islam practiced in America as an offshoot of the Nation of Islam. Five-percenters came to be known as the followers of the teachings of Clarence 13X. Many emcees from the mid-1980s to mid-1990s are adherents to Five-percenter knowledge and teachings.

"Suleiman al-Faris" was John Walker Lindh's chosen name after his conversion to Islam.

"last letter home" contains parts of John Walker's Lindh's statement to the court as he was sentenced to prison in October 2002.

About the Author

© Rebekah Raleigh

Kevin Coval is the author of *Slingshots* and *Everyday People*, and cofounder and artistic director of Louder Than a Bomb: The Chicago Youth Poetry Festival. A regular contributor to Chicago Public Radio and a four-time HBO Def Poet, Coval teaches in schools around Chicago.